basic flavorings
Ginger

basic flavorings

Ginger

Clare Gordon-Smith

photography by

James Merrell

COURAGE
BOOKS

AN IMPRINT OF RUNNING PRESS
PHILADELPHIA · LONDON

Art Director **Jacqui Small**

Art Editor **Penny Stock**

Designer **Megan Smith**

Editor **Elsa Petersen-Schepelern**

Photography **James Merrell**

Food Stylist **Clare Gordon-Smith**

Stylist **Sue Parker**

Production Manager **Kate Mackillop**

Printed and bound in Hong Kong

10 9 8 7 6 5 4 3 2 1
Digit on the right indicates the number of this printing

Library of Congress Cataloging-in-Publication number
97-66813

ISBN 0-7624-0199-0

This edition published in the United States of America in 1998 by
Courage Books, an imprint of
Running Press Book Publishers
125 South Twenty-second Street
Philadelphia, Pennsylvania 19103-4399

**My thanks to my family—my father,
sister, and grandmother—to David
Hurcomb, Sarah Kidd, Annabel
Ford, Di Reeds, Rosemary Scoular
and Vanessa Kearns, James
Merrell, Sue Parker, Dinny Hall, and
the team at Ryland Peters & Small.**

Notes:
Ovens should be preheated to the
specified temperature—if using a
convection oven, adjust time and
temperature according to the
manufacturer's instructions.

The recipe for Tomato Chile Jam on
page 44 is reprinted with permission
from Chef Peter Gordon, author of
The Sugar Club Cookbook, published
by Hodder & Stoughton, 1997.

Ginger is one of the most ancient of all flavorings, used in the early civilizations of China and India, and by the Romans. The Spanish took it to the West Indies, and the Portuguese to West Africa, while in modern times it is used in one guise or another in almost every cuisine. Ginger is available in several forms; **fresh gingerroot** is usually peeled then sliced or grated (add a dash of lemon juice or vinegar to stop it browning). Before the advent of refrigeration and fast transport, many ways were found to keep this valuable spice—**preserved stem ginger** in sugar syrup, **crystallized ginger**, **dried ginger**, pink Japanese **pickled ginger** preserved in vinegar, or dried **ground ginger** (Jamaican ground ginger is thought to be the best). **Ginger wine**, similar to sherry, is wonderful in sauces, giving just a hint of flavor. Two botanical "cousins" of ginger, **galangal** (second from right) and **krachai** (second from left), also known as "Chinese keys," are available fresh, dried, or ground, and have a brighter, sharper, aromatic flavor. They are widely used in Southeast Asian cooking.

ginger wine

krachai

Japanese pickled ginger

chopped dried ginger

the *flavors of*
Ginger

galangal

fresh gingerroot

crystallized ginger

ground ginger

preserved stem
ginger in syrup

oriental marinade

Thai dipping sauce

As well as appearing alone as a flavoring ingredient, ginger also stars in some famous spice mixtures, both fresh and dried. From left is a typical **oriental marinade**, consisting of soy sauce, ginger, honey, and garlic—the honey helps it stick to the food. Ginger also appears in the

Chinese Trinity of flavorings, with garlic and spring onions, and in the Thai Triad, consisting of ginger, garlic, and chiles. The **Thai dipping sauce** includes ginger, chiles, shallots, soft brown sugar, and rice vinegar. Make **ginger vinegar** or **ginger juice** by

ginger vinegar
or ginger juice

Japanese
pickled ginger

pickling spice

mixed spice

steeping sliced ginger in rice vinegar or sherry vinegar—wonderful in dressings and marinades. **Mixed spice**—used to flavor cakes, breads, and desserts—consists of ginger, coriander seeds, and cinnamon, and may also include other spices such as cardamom and cloves.

Pickling spice is used for all kinds of savory pickles from gherkins to chutneys. Its precise composition varies around the world, but may include ginger, cinnamon, chiles, peppercorns, bay leaf, allspice, juniper berries, fennel seeds, and mustard seeds, all in their dried form.

Salads

Pacific ginger salad

Pacific-Rim cooking in California, Australia, and New Zealand melds the influences of European, Latin American, and Asian cuisines in the most exciting way. Scallops or crab could be used in this salad instead of the salmon and shrimp. Serve it as an appetizer or increase the quantity to make an entree.

Place the spinach in a bowl, slice the papaya and avocado, then add the mooli, shrimp, and salmon. Mix the dressing ingredients together and pour over the salad. Sprinkle with sesame seeds and serve.

1 lb. baby spinach

1 papaya, peeled and seeded

1 avocado, peeled and stoned

4 oz. mooli (Japanese white radish), sliced

8 oz. cooked shrimp, peeled

2 oz. smoked salmon slices

toasted sesame seeds, to serve

ginger dressing

3 tablespoons soy sauce

2 tablespoons rice vinegar

1 tablespoon sunflower oil

1 garlic clove, crushed

1–2 tablespoons Japanese pickled ginger

Serves 4

Citus carrot salad
with ginger dressing

Carrot and orange is a favorite combination
in many cuisines, but a little dash of ginger
in the dressing gives this salad a subtle
oriental twist that is very refreshing. It's a
great salad to serve with baked potatoes or
a creamy-cheese pasta. Watercress will give
a peppery edge to the salad, but you could
substitute other green salad leaves.

To prepare the dressing, mix all the ingredients until
thoroughly combined, then set aside.
Place the watercress in a salad bowl, arrange the
grated carrots and orange segments on top, pour
over the dressing, and serve.

about 2 oz. watercress

1 lb. crisp young
carrots, grated

3 oranges, peeled
and segmented

ginger dressing

3½ tablespoons ginger
vinegar (see page 8–9)
or 1 inch fresh
gingerroot, grated,
then mixed with
3½ tablespoons white
rice vinegar

½ teaspoon
wholegrain mustard

1 teaspoon honey

grated rind and juice
of 1 medium orange

3 tablespoons olive oil

2 tablespoons toasted
sesame seeds

sea salt and freshly
ground black pepper

Serves 4

a fresh summer salad with a

spicy oriental twist to the dressing

Ginger chicken salad
with honeydew melon and celery

Melon and ginger is a classic combination—
and a wonderful, refreshing addition to this
traditional chicken salad.

2 tablespoons olive oil

2 celery stalks,
finely chopped

2 shallots,
roughly chopped

½ teaspoon
cayenne pepper

1 honeydew melon

1 cooked chicken

4 tablespoons
homemade mayonnaise

6 tablespoons
sour cream

6 pieces crystallized
ginger, chopped

to serve

green salad leaves

paprika, to sprinkle

Serves 4

Heat the olive oil in a skillet, add the celery and
shallots, and gently sauté until soft. Stir in the
cayenne pepper. Let cool, then chill.
Cut the melon in half, remove and discard the seeds,
and cut the flesh into cubes with a knife, or into balls
using a melon-baller or teaspoon. (Hold the melon
over a bowl to catch the juice.)
Shred the chicken into bite-sized pieces and place in
a bowl. Add the melon, celery, and shallots, then stir
in the mayonnaise, sour cream, and ginger.
Place the salad leaves on a salad platter, spoon on
the chicken, sprinkle with paprika, and serve.

Summer salad
with chile and ginger dressing

Change the ingredients in this salad
according to what's fresh and exciting in the
shops. Use chicken, turkey, or beef, and
leaves like baby spinach or lambs' lettuce.
Marinate the chicken for as long as you have
available, from 30 minutes to overnight.
Chinese chives are sold in Asian markets,
but if you can't find them, use ordinary
chives or parsley instead.

Toast the cashews in a dry skillet until lightly golden.
Transfer to a small bowl and set aside.
To make the marinade, grate the zest of the orange
and squeeze the juice into a bowl. Stir in the
remaining marinade ingredients, add the chicken,
and turn to coat. Marinate for 1 hour or overnight.
Mix the dressing ingredients together and set aside.
Shred the spinach and radicchio leaves and put in a
bowl. Slice the shiitakes, if using, and scallions and
add to the bowl together with the watercress, basil,
snipped Chinese chives, and toasted cashews, then
transfer to a salad bowl.
Heat the oil in a skillet, remove the chicken from
the marinade, drain (reserving the marinade), then
gently sauté the chicken until cooked—about
4 minutes. Stir in the marinade ingredients and
simmer for a few minutes. Arrange the chicken over
the salad leaves, pour over the dressing and
lukewarm marinade, then serve.

⅓ cup cashews

12 oz. chicken, trimmed
and cut in 2-inch strips

8 oz. baby spinach

8 oz. radicchio

8 oz. fresh shiitake
mushrooms (optional)

8 scallions

1 bunch watercress

12 basil leaves

2 oz. Chinese chives

corn oil, for cooking

chile marinade

1 orange

3 tablespoons soy sauce

1 tablespoon sugar

4 tablespoons chile oil

ginger dressing

3 tablespoons chile oil

3 tablespoons sherry

2 tablespoons ginger
vinegar (page 8)

1 tablespoon corn oil

Serves 4

Salads **17**

Appetizers

Herbed duck rolls
with ginger and plum sauce

A spectacular appetizer for an informal
dinner. Either assemble the rolls for your
guests, or set out the prepared ingredients
and let them make their own packages.

To make the crêpes, sift the flour and salt into a bowl
and make a well in the center. Drop the eggs into the
well and beat thoroughly. Gradually beat in enough
milk to make the mixture smooth and creamy. Stir in
the chives and let stand for about 10 minutes.
For the filling, prick the duck breasts with a fork,
brush the skin with honey, sprinkle with ginger and
soy sauce, then cook in a preheated oven at 375°F
for 15 to 20 minutes.
Heat a crêpe pan or small skillet, brush with a little
melted butter, then add a ladle of batter, rotating the
pan so the base is coated with a thin layer. Cook
until the underside is golden brown, loosen the
edges, flip with a palette knife, and cook until the
other side is golden. Repeat with the remaining
batter until you have 8 to 10 crêpes. Stack them as
you go, placing a layer of wax paper between each
and keeping them warm in a low oven.
To serve, slice the duck breast crosswise. Spread a
spoonful of hoisin sauce on each crêpe, add some
cucumber, scallions, and a couple of slices of duck
on each. Fold the crêpes into a package and tie up
each one with a chive. Serve with soy sauce.

2 duck breasts

2 tablespoons honey

1 inch fresh gingerroot,
peeled and grated

2 teaspoons soy sauce,
plus extra, to serve

2 tablespoons
hoisin sauce

½ cucumber, cut into
strips lengthwise

8 scallions,
sliced lengthwise

1 bunch fresh chives

2–4 tablespoons
melted butter

herbed crêpes

1 cup all-purpose flour

a pinch of salt

2 eggs

⅔–¾ cup milk

2 tablespoons
chopped fresh chives

Serves 4

Seafood noodle soup

For a light ginger flavor, peel the fresh
gingerroot, grate it, and infuse in the stock.
For a stronger flavor, infuse the peel as well.
Galangal or krachai could be used instead of
the ginger to give a subtly different flavor.

Peel and slice the ginger, reserving the peel if
preferred. Pour the stock into a large saucepan and
bring to a boil. Add the soy sauce, fish sauce, sugar,
lemongrass, sliced ginger, and peel (optional), and
simmer gently for 10 to 20 minutes to develop the
flavors. Strain into a bowl then return to the rinsed
pan. Bring to just below boiling point, add the fish and
seafood, then simmer for 8 minutes more, or until the
fish is just cooked, and the shrimp turn pink.
Break the trout fillets into large pieces, add the
noodles, return to a boil, then serve in small
Chinese-style bowls, sprinkled with sliced scallions,
and sprigs of cilantro.

1 inch fresh gingerroot,
peeled and sliced

2 cups chicken stock

3 tablespoons
light soy sauce

1 tablespoon
Thai fish sauce

2 teaspoons brown
sugar or palm sugar

½ stalk lemongrass,
lightly crushed

14 oz. trout fillets

8 uncooked shrimp,
peeled and deveined

6 oz. crabmeat
(optional)

1 sheet Chinese
rice noodles

to serve

3 scallions,
sliced diagonally

sprigs of cilantro

Serves 4

ginger, galangal, and krachai—all used in Thai cooking—give **subtly different tastes**

Ginger tomato soup
with garlic and cayenne pepper

Tomato soup made with ginger and cayenne
has more "kick" than one made with herbs.
Use good, ripe, red tomatoes—I find vine-
ripened ones have the best flavor. If serving
this soup to vegetarians, use vegetable stock
instead of chicken, but whichever kind you
use, always try to find the real thing, rather
than using cubes—these days, even
supermarkets sell real stock in plastic tubs.

Peel the tomatoes by plunging them in boiling water
for 1 minute, then slip off the skins and discard.
Coarsely chop the flesh.
Heat the oil in a saucepan, add the onion, and gently
sauté until soft and translucent. Add the tomatoes,
garlic, ginger, sugar, cayenne, salt, pepper, and
vegetable or chicken stock. Bring to a boil and
simmer for 20 minutes until just tender.
Serve, sprinkled with sprigs of rosemary.

Variation:
If you prefer a smooth soup, puree in a blender or
food processor before serving, though I prefer the
coarser, more homemade look of the original soup.

1 lb. plum tomatoes

2 tablespoons olive oil

1 onion, finely chopped

1 garlic clove, crushed

1 inch fresh gingerroot,
peeled and grated

a pinch of brown sugar

a pinch of
cayenne pepper

2½ cups vegetable or
chicken stock

sea salt and freshly
ground black pepper

sprigs of rosemary,
to serve

Serves 4

Carrot and ginger pots

Another great combination of ginger and carrots—these delicate little pots make a light summer dish, and can be made in advance. When cooking with ricotta cheese, always use it the day you buy it. Serve with sourdough bread and a crisp green salad.

⅓ cup almonds, blanched and peeled

8 oz. young carrots

1 cup ricotta cheese

1 egg, beaten

1 inch fresh gingerroot, peeled and grated

1 tablespoon chopped fresh parsley

1 tablespoon olive oil

sea salt and freshly ground black pepper

Serves 4

Roughly chop the almonds and set aside. Finely grate the carrots. Break the ricotta into a bowl and beat in the other ingredients to form a smooth mixture. Season, then spoon into ramekin dishes. Put the dishes into a bain-marie and cook in a preheated oven at 350°F for 40 minutes until just set and firm. Serve warm or chilled.

Melon with ginger

A modern update of an old-fashioned dish.

1 honeydew melon, halved and seeded

2 oranges

4 oz. crystallized ginger, chopped

confectioners sugar, to taste

Serves 4

Scoop out the melon flesh with a melon baller or small teaspoon. Divide between small individual glasses or place in one large glass bowl. Remove the orange peel with a zester and blanch the peel in boiling water for 2 minutes. Drain. Using a serrated knife, segment the oranges, discarding the pith. Add the orange and ginger to the melon. Sprinkle with a little sugar and orange zest and serve.

Roasted ginger salmon
with bok choy and tabbouleh salad

This must be the ultimate in Fusion Food! Tabbouleh salad comes from the Middle East, but has Thai flavorings. The salmon is roasted with Chinese ingredients, including bok choy, which is now widely available. The result is absolutely delectable!

Place the salmon pieces in a roasting pan. Brush with the lemon juice, sprinkle with salt, chile powder, and ginger and roast in a preheated oven at 400°F for about 5 minutes.

To make the tabbouleh salad, place the couscous in a bowl, pour over 1¼ cups boiling water, stir in the fish sauce, and let soak for 10 minutes.

Finely slice the cucumber diagonally, making the pieces as long as possible. Place the scallions, beans, and cucumber in a bowl and sprinkle over the rice vinegar. Fork through the couscous.

Heat a small skillet or wok, add the corn oil and, when hot, stir-fry the bok choy and Thai seven-spice for a few minutes until the leaves are slightly wilted.

To serve, spoon the tabbouleh salad onto heated plates, add the bok choy, then top with the salmon.

4 salmon fillets, cut into narrow slices

1 tablespoon lemon juice

a pinch of salt

a pinch of chile powder

1 inch fresh gingerroot, thinly sliced

1 tablespoon corn oil

4 baby bok choy

2 teaspoons Thai seven-spice

tabbouleh salad

¾ cup easy-cook couscous

1 tablespoon Thai fish sauce

1 cucumber, peeled and seeded

5 scallions, finely sliced diagonally

6 oz. green beans, finely sliced diagonally

2 tablespoons rice vinegar

Serves 4

Five-spice snapper
with pineapple passionfruit salsa

Chinese five-spice powder is highly aromatic, with star anise as its major component. The remaining four spices are cinnamon, cloves, szechuan pepper, and fennel seed. The hot and sweet crystallized ginger in the salsa is a fine complement to those flavors.

To prepare the topping for the fish, heat the oil in a small skillet, add the onion and garlic, and sauté gently for 5 minutes. Remove from the heat and stir in the five-spice, ground almonds, breadcrumbs, chopped parsley, and chopped nuts.
Place the fish in a greased roasting pan, spread the mixture on top of each fillet, and cook in a preheated oven at 375°F for 10 to 15 minutes.
Meanwhile, to make the salsa, scoop the passionfruit flesh into a small bowl, add the pineapple and crystallized ginger, stir well, and use to pack the passionfruit shells.
Serve with the fish.

4 snapper fillets

2 tablespoons olive oil

1 onion, finely chopped

1 large garlic clove, chopped

2 teaspoons Chinese five-spice

4 tablespoons ground almonds

6 tablespoons dry white breadcrumbs

3 tablespoons chopped fresh flat-leaf parsley

¼ cup chopped nuts

pineapple passionfruit salsa

2 passionfruit, halved, shells reserved

4 oz. pineapple, fresh or canned, finely chopped

4 pieces crystallized ginger, chopped

Serves 4

a modern update on

the Antipodes—serve

Ginger-roasted chicken
with red bell peppers and pumpkin

A Pacific-Rim recipe—Australians and New Zealanders love baked pumpkin with their Sunday roast. And they love spicy flavors from around the world—this time ginger and spicy jerk seasoning from the Caribbean. The latter is available in Afro-Caribbean stores and some supermarkets, but if you can't find it, substitute hot chile sauce.

Put the peppers, pumpkin, onion, and chile in a roasting pan and sprinkle with the ginger, orange zest, and juice. Put the chicken on top and sprinkle with jerk seasoning. Cook in a preheated oven at 400°F, basting every 20 minutes, for about 1 hour or until the juices run clear when the thickest part of the thigh is pierced with a skewer.
Transfer the chicken and vegetables to a serving plate and keep them warm. Strain off the fat from the pan, pour in the stock, bring to a boil, and simmer for about 10 minutes on top of the stove until reduced by half. Serve with the vegetables and boiled wild rice or a mixture of basmati and wild rice.

1 yellow bell pepper, halved, seeded, and cut into chunks

1 red bell pepper, halved, seeded, and cut into chunks

1 lb. pumpkin or butternut squash, sliced, seeded, and peeled

1 red onion, cut into wedges

1 red chile, halved, seeded, and thinly sliced

1 inch fresh gingerroot, peeled and grated

juice and grated zest of 1 orange

1 chicken, about 3 lb.

2 teaspoons Jamaican jerk seasoning

1¼ cups chicken stock

Serves 4

aditional Sunday roast from

th **baked pumpkin**

Lemon chicken
with saffron spiced yogurt

A top London jewelry designer showed me
this recipe for a story I did for *Marie Claire*
about designers who entertained at home.
We found that many fashion designers are
passionately interested in food and cooking.
If you don't have a chicken brick, use any
large, ovenproof casserole dish.

Put the lemon and orange inside the chicken. Make
small cuts in the chicken skin with a sharp knife and
insert the garlic and ginger slices. Place the chicken
in a soaked chicken brick and sprinkle with paprika.
Pour the yogurt in a bowl and add the saffron, salt,
and olive oil. With a mortar and pestle, crush the
coriander seeds, the black seeds from the cardamom
pods, and the green peppercorns, then stir into the
yogurt. Pour the yogurt mixture over the chicken, put
the lid on the brick and place in a cold oven.
Turn the heat to 400°F and cook for about 1½ to
2 hours or until the chicken is tender.
Serve with rice or vegetables.

a spicy chicken variation on

traditional **roast lamb** spiked with garlic

1 lemon, peeled

½ orange, peeled

1 chicken, about 3 lb.

1 garlic clove, sliced

1 inch fresh gingerroot,
peeled and sliced

a pinch of paprika

¾ cup plain yogurt

a good pinch
of saffron threads

a pinch of salt

2 tablespoons
light olive oil

1 heaped teaspoon
coriander seeds

3 heaped teaspoons
green cardamom pods

1 teaspoon green
peppercorns

Serves 4

Barbecued chicken
on a ciabatta salad sandwich

This is a quick and easy but very flavorful recipe for chicken pieces. Serve it with salad or steamed or stir-fried vegetables as an entree for lunch or a simple dinner—or as a filling for a special sandwich, as here.

4 chicken pieces

ginger marinade

8 tablespoons tomato ketchup

2 tablespoons red wine vinegar

1 inch fresh gingerroot, peeled and grated

1 garlic clove, crushed

to serve

1 loaf ciabatta bread

butter

salad leaves

2 ripe red Italian plum tomatoes, sliced

salt and pepper

Serves 4

Mix the marinade ingredients in a shallow dish, add the chicken, turn to coat well, and set aside in the refrigerator for up to 1 hour.

Remove the chicken from the marinade and char-grill on both sides until tender. Alternatively, place the chicken in a roasting pan and bake in a preheated oven at 400°F for 10 to 15 minutes until just cooked. Remove from the oven or grill and slice on a board, discarding the bones if any.

To serve as a sandwich, cut the ciabatta in half lengthwise, butter lightly, fill with salad leaves, sliced tomatoes, and the chicken, then season and serve.

Stir-fried ginger beef
with noodles and oriental vegetables

Many classic Chinese stir-fry dishes begin by sautéing the Chinese Trinity of flavorings—scallions, ginger, and garlic. This one omits the garlic, and uses the ginger in the dressing rather than the stir-fry. It's a novel twist on a traditional combination.

First, prepare carrot curls by pulling a vegetable peeler down the length of the carrot. Arrange them in curls and leave for a few minutes in ice water. Cut the sugarsnap peas in half diagonally. Cut the scallions diagonally into ½-inch slices. To make the sesame dressing, mix all the ingredients together in a small bowl. Place the noodles in a second bowl, pour over boiling water, let soak for a few minutes, then drain. Heat the oil in a skillet or wok, then add the strips of beef, and stir-fry for about 2 minutes. Add the vegetables and stir-fry for 5 minutes more. Sprinkle with the sesame dressing and serve immediately with the noodles.

2 carrots

2 oz. sugarsnap peas, topped and tailed

1 bunch scallions

8 oz. Chinese egg noodles

1 tablespoon vegetable oil

1 lb. beef fillet, cut into strips about 1 x 2 inches

sesame dressing

1 inch fresh gingerroot, peeled and finely shredded

2 tablespoons light soy sauce

1 tablespoon rice wine vinegar

2 teaspoons chile oil

2 tablespoons sesame seeds

Serves 4

a quick and easy stir-fry—perfect served with steamed rice or **Chinese noodles**

Gingered pork fillets
with a ginger applesauce

Pork and apple is a traditional combination, and popular even with people who don't much like meat served with fruit. This sauce is also wonderful with venison or duck.

To make the marinade, mix the honey in a bowl with the white wine vinegar, soy sauce, and grated fresh ginger. Stir well.

Slice the pork fillets diagonally, add to the marinade, turn to coat, cover, and refrigerate for at least 4 hours or overnight.

Put 2 tablespoons cold water and half the sugar into a saucepan and cook, stirring, over a low heat until the sugar is dissolved.

Add the apple, sherry, ground ginger, the remaining sugar, salt, and pepper, then cover and stew gently until just tender.

Transfer the sliced pork to a roasting pan and add 2 tablespoons cold water.

Roast in a preheated oven at 400°F for 15 to 20 minutes until just tender, then transfer to a heated serving dish together with the apples.

Blanch the Chinese egg noodles in boiling water for 1 minute, or according to the package instructions, then drain, toss in a little sesame oil, and serve with the pork and apples.

2 lb. pork fillets

½ cup sugar

1 lb. apples, peeled, cored, and sliced

1 tablespoon sherry

a pinch of ground ginger

salt and freshly ground black pepper

ginger marinade

3 tablespoons honey

2 tablespoons white wine vinegar

1 tablespoon soy sauce

2 teaspoons grated fresh gingerroot

to serve

Chinese egg noodles

sesame oil

Serves 4

Mango pork kebabs
in orange and ginger marinade

Broiled or barbecued kebabs make a great
quick and easy dish, packed with zippy flavor
from the ginger marinade—and marinated
meats are always wonderful on the barbecue.
Serve with a spicy rice salad and peppery
watercress dressed with vinaigrette.

Mix the marinade ingredients in a shallow dish.
Add the pork strips to the marinade, turn to coat
well, and marinate in the refrigerator for 1 to 2 hours.
To assemble the kebabs, thread the pork, mango,
and onions onto pre-soaked bamboo kebab sticks.
Cook under a preheated broiler for about 10 minutes,
turning several times, then serve immediately.

1½ lb. pork tenderloin,
sliced crosswise
into ½-inch strips

2 mangoes, sliced

4 red onions, sliced

sea salt and freshly
ground black pepper

**orange and
ginger marinade**

1 teaspoon
ground cumin

⅔ cup orange juice

1 teaspoon orange zest

½ cup olive oil

1 teaspoon lime zest

2 tablespoons freshly
squeezed lime juice

1 shallot, chopped

1 inch fresh gingerroot,
peeled and grated

1 bunch fresh
cilantro leaves

Serves 4

a ginger-orange marinade tenderizes

the pork and packs it **full of flavor**

Accompaniments

Ginger apple chutney

Chutneys are the wonderful spicy savory preserves that India has contributed to the rest of the world. Chutneys taste particularly good with cold meats and cheese, and contain various spices, both aromatic and hot. This one is spicy, but not overly so.

Put the apples in a non-aluminum pan with the treacle or corn syrup and 1¼ cups of the vinegar. Cook over a medium heat until thick and pulpy. Stir in the remaining vinegar, followed by the sugar, ginger, mixed spice, cayenne, raisins, salt, and pepper. Cook for a further 5 minutes, or until thick. Bottle in sterilized jars. Cover and label.

3½ lb. cooking apples, peeled, cored, and chopped

1 tablespoon treacle or dark corn syrup

2 cups cider vinegar

2½ cups brown sugar

1 inch fresh gingerroot, peeled and chopped

a pinch of mixed spice (see page 9)

a pinch of cayenne pepper

½ teaspoon salt

3 cups seedless raisins

black and white pepper

Makes 3 jars of 1 pint

Tomato chile jam

This chile jam is a signature dish from one of London's most innovative chefs—New Zealander Peter Gordon of the Sugar Club Restaurant in Notting Hill. This is a great relish to keep in the fridge, and good with chicken, fish, and pork, or spread on toast with goat cheese and arugula leaves.

Put the chiles, garlic, ginger, fish sauce, and half the tomatoes in a blender and whizz to a fine puree. Cut the remaining tomatoes into fine dice and set aside. Place the puree, sugar, and vinegar into a deep saucepan and bring gently to a boil, stirring constantly. When it reaches boiling point, reduce to a gentle simmer, add the diced tomatoes, and skim off any foam that rises to the surface. Cook for about 30 to 45 minutes, stirring from time to time to release the solids that settle on the base. Scrape the sides of the pot during cooking. Pour the jam into warmed, sterilized glass jars and let cool to room temperature. Seal with lids and store in the refrigerator. Use within 1 month.

4 red chiles, such as serranos

4 garlic cloves

1 inch fresh gingerroot, peeled and roughly chopped

3½ tablespoons Thai fish sauce

1 lb. very ripe red cherry tomatoes

1½ cups sugar

½ cup red wine vinegar

Makes 3 jars of ½ pint

Rhubarb ginger jam

Rhubarb and ginger is a classic combination, and if forced rhubarb is in season, this delicate jam will be a very pretty pink.

6 lb. rhubarb, cut into 2-inch lengths

rind and juice of 2 lemons

5 oz. fresh gingerroot, lightly crushed

6 lb. sugar

Makes 3 jars of 2 pints

Put the rhubarb in a preserving pan. Tie up the lemon rind and crushed ginger in cheesecloth and add to the pan. Bring slowly to a boil, then simmer until tender (about 8 minutes), stirring as necessary. Stir in the lemon juice and sugar until dissolved, then boil for about 10 minutes. To test for setting, put 1 teaspoon jam on a cold saucer. Wait for 5 minutes, then push with your finger. If the surface wrinkles, the jam is set. If not, boil a few minutes longer. Pour into sterilized jars, seal, and use within 4 months.

Cranberry conserve
with apples and ginger

A sweet and sour, spicy and savory accompaniment for game or poultry.

1 lb. apples, peeled, cored and diced

1 tablespoon sugar

1 cup maple syrup

1 lb. cranberries

grated zest of 1 orange

1 inch fresh gingerroot, peeled and grated

Makes 3 jars of ½ pint

Put the apples, sugar, and 2 tablespoons water in a pan and shake to stop the apples sticking. Mix in the maple syrup, cranberries, orange zest, and ginger and cook at a high heat. When the berries begin to burst, reduce the heat to low, cover, stir occasionally, and cook for 10 minutes. Pour into sterilized jars, then seal and use within 4 months.

Desserts

Plum berry compote
with lime leaves and ginger

A compote is a gentle stew of fresh fruits, served alone or with cream or ice-cream. Use single fruits, or a combination or fruits—this one uses all-red varieties. The subtle ginger syrup gives it a spicy bright taste.

Halve and stone the plums, trim and cut the rhubarb into 1-inch pieces, and pick over the raspberries. Put the sugar and water in a saucepan, heat gently to dissolve the sugar, then bring to a boil and simmer for 5 minutes.

Add the lime leaves, if using, then stir in the ginger and ginger wine and allow to infuse for 30 minutes. Stir in the fruit and simmer for 7 to 10 minutes until the fruit is just soft but still holds its shape. Remove the lime leaves and serve with crème fraîche and cookies such as the Ginger Shortbread on page 62.

1 lb. plums

1 lb. rhubarb

1¾ cups raspberries

⅔ cup sugar

½ cup water

3 kaffir lime leaves
(optional)

2 oz. preserved
stem ginger, chopped

3 tablespoons ginger
wine (or 1 tablespoon
sherry mixed with
2 tablespoons orange
juice and 1 teaspoon
grated gingerroot)

Serves 4

Steamed puddings
with ginger and apricot

Steamed puddings are the perfect comfort food, and you can make them with any number of variations. I often cook them in ovenproof cups or molds which look very pretty, though you can also make a large one. When made in small dariole molds, they are called "Castle Puddings."

To make the topping, melt the butter in a small pan, stir in the sugar and honey, and heat until dissolved.

Divide the apricot halves between 6 well-buttered ramekin dishes, teacups, molds, or a 2–pint pudding basin. Arrange them, curved side down, then spoon in the melted topping mixture.

To make the sponge, cream the butter and sugar until soft and creamy. Gradually beat in the eggs, then fold in the flour, ginger, and crystallized ginger. Spoon on top of the apricots, then cover each dish with a piece of wax paper a little larger than the molds. Secure with string.

Place in large pan of boiling water so the water comes half way up the sides of the molds, then simmer for about 1 hour.

Serve with a vanilla custard.

apricot topping

4 tablespoons
sweet butter

¼ cup brown sugar

2 tablespoons honey

10 oz. canned apricot
halves, drained

ginger sponge

½ cup sweet butter,
softened

⅔ cup caster sugar

2 eggs

¾ cup self-rising flour

1 teaspoon
ground ginger

3 oz. crystallized
ginger, chopped

Serves 4

Ginger bavarois
with honey and chocolate

Bavarois mousses make very classic and elegant puddings. Though simple, they need a little patience to make, but are always worth the trouble. Whipped cream is folded into a traditional custard, which is then set with gelatine. Leaf gelatine is now widely available and I find it much easier to use.

Place the milk and almonds in a pan and bring to just below boiling point. Remove from the heat, stir in the ginger wine, and leave to infuse for 10 minutes. Beat the egg yolks and sugar until light and fluffy (about 3–4 minutes). Stir in the hot milk and honey. Return the custard to the pan and heat gently, stirring, until thickened—do not allow to boil or the mixture will curdle.

Dissolve the gelatine according to the package instructions. Fold the gelatine into the custard, fill a bowl with ice, and set the pan of custard on top. Beat the custard until almost set. Lightly whip the cream and fold into the custard. Pour the mixture into 6 small molds or 1 large one and leave to set in the refrigerator for a few hours.

To serve, gently melt the chocolate over a pan of simmering water. Invert the molds onto individual serving plates and spoon some cream around the bavarois. Drizzle the melted chocolate over the pudding and sprinkle with toasted flaked almonds and preserved ginger.

1½ cups full-cream milk

⅔ cup blanched almonds, coarsely chopped

4 tablespoons ginger wine (or 1½ tablespoons sherry, 2½ tablespoons orange juice, and 1 teaspoon ground ginger)

4 egg yolks

4 tablespoons sugar

2 tablespoons honey

5 sheets gelatine

¾ cup heavy cream

to serve

2 oz. bitter chocolate, melted

4–8 tablespoons light cream

¼ cup flaked almonds, toasted

2 oz. preserved stem ginger, cut into pieces

Serves 4

Gingered berry tarts

Crystallizing is one of the oldest forms of preserving ginger, and is therefore found in many traditional recipes, especially for treats such as puddings and cakes.

To make the pastry, mix the flour and sugar in a bowl, then rub in the butter until it resembles bread crumbs. Fold in the egg yolks and just enough water to bind the mixture (about 1 to 2 teaspoons). Wrap the pastry in plastic wrap or foil and chill for about 30 minutes.

Roll out the pastry on a floured surface and use to line eight 4-inch false-bottomed tart pans. Trim the edges, then chill for 30 minutes. Line the pastry with foil or parchment paper and fill with dried beans or ceramic baking beans. Cook in a preheated oven at 400°F for 10 to15 minutes until lightly browned at the edges. Remove from the oven and remove the parchment paper and baking beans.

To make the pastry cream, beat the eggs, egg yolks, and sugar in a bowl. In another bowl, beat the cornstarch and milk until smooth, beat in the heavy cream, then beat into the egg mixture. Bring gently to a boil on top of the stove, then turn down the heat and cook, stirring, until thickened. Let cool, then spoon into the pastry cases, top with the fruit and ginger, and serve. Remove from the oven, top with the fruit and ginger, then serve hot or at room temperature.

1 cup plus 2 tablespoons all-purpose flour, sifted

4 tablespoons sugar

6 tablespoons sweet butter

2 egg yolks

a little ice water

pastry cream

2 eggs

2 egg yolks

2 tablespoons cornstarch

¾ cup warm milk

1¼ cups heavy cream

berry topping

4 oz. blueberries or wild strawberries

4 oz. raspberries or pitted cherries

4 pieces crystallized or preserved ginger, sliced or chopped

8 whole cherries, with stalks (optional)

Serves 8

Gingered tea granita

A granita is a frozen liquid, mashed into small pieces before serving. It is softer than a sorbet, but not as smooth. This is a frozen version of Chinese ginger tea, often served at the end of a meal to aid digestion—in fact ginger tea is well-known throughout Asia as a good way to soothe an upset stomach.

2¾ cups water

1½ cups sugar

2 inches fresh gingerroot, peeled and sliced

zest and juice of 1 lemon

Serves 4

Put the water and sugar in a saucepan and heat gently until the sugar has dissolved. Simmer gently for 3 minutes.

Add the ginger, lemon zest, and juice to the simmering water and leave to infuse for 20 minutes. Strain and serve as tea, or cool and freeze. To serve, allow to thaw a little for about 15 to 30 minutes, then scoop into serving dishes with a small teaspoon.

a soft sorbet with a thrilling zippy edge to its **icy, spicy flavor**

Ginger ice-cream
with crystallized ginger and cherries

Ginger is the perfect ingredient for ices and ice-creams. Cold dulls flavor, but the strength of ginger is robust enough to survive the freezing process.

Place the milk and ground ginger in a heavy-bottom saucepan and heat to simmering point. Beat the egg yolks and sugar together in a large mixing bowl until thick and pale yellow in color (about 3 to 4 minutes). Gradually pour the hot milk into the egg mixture, stirring all the time.

Strain the mixture into a heavy-bottom or double saucepan and stir over a gentle heat until the custard thickens enough to coat the back of a wooden spoon. Do not allow to boil or the mixture will curdle. Pour into a large mixing bowl and let cool. Beat the cream until it forms soft peaks, then fold into the custard. Pour into a freezer container and freeze for about 1 hour.

Stir the crystallized ginger and glacé cherries into the ice-cream and return it to the freezer for 1 hour more. Beat, cover, seal, and freeze. If using an ice-cream maker, do not beat the cream, but stir into the egg mixture just before churning. Churn, stir in the ginger and cherries, then serve immediately or freeze. If frozen hard, transfer to the refrigerator for about 20 minutes before serving.

1¾ cups whole milk

1 teaspoon ground ginger

4 egg yolks

6 tablespoons sugar

⅔ cup heavy cream

3 oz. or 6 pieces crystallized or stem ginger, finely chopped

1 oz. or 2 tablespoons glacé cherries, (optional)

Serves 4

creamy, spic

ice-crear

astes in this sumptuous

orm the **perfect finale** for a great dinner

Baking

Gingerbread

Gingerbread has been popular for centuries and is thought to have been introduced to Europe at the time of the Crusades. It is a very easy recipe—the liquid ingredients are heated together in a pan, then all the dry ingredients are added, followed by the beaten egg. Serve it plain, or drizzle over the light lemon glaze from the recipe on page 60.

1 stick butter

½ cup plus
2 tablespoons
brown sugar

⅔ cup full-cream milk

4 oz. light molasses
or dark corn syrup

4 oz. honey
or light corn syrup

1⅔ cups
all-purpose flour

3–4 teaspoons
ground ginger

1 teaspoon
baking soda

1 large egg, beaten

Makes 16

Grease and line an 8-inch square cake pan.
Melt the butter, sugar, milk, molasses and honey in a saucepan over a low heat, stirring all the time.
Remove from the heat and cool until lukewarm.
Sift the dry ingredients and stir into the liquid.
Beat in the beaten egg, mixing until smooth, then spoon the mixture into the prepared pan.
Bake in a preheated oven at 300°F for about 1¼ to 1½ hours until cooked, or when a cocktail stick is inserted and comes out clean.
Cool for 5 minutes on a wire rack, then turn out of the pan onto the rack and cool completely.
Cut the gingerbread into 16 pieces and serve immediately, or transfer to an airtight container and eat within 1 week.

Ginger cake

This wonderful, old-fashioned cake recipe was found in a very old cookbook. It's the kind of cake our grannies used to make— tried and tested, by people who really knew the secret of successful baking!

Grease and line a 9-inch deep ring mold. Cream the butter and sugar together (about 10 minutes), then gradually beat in the eggs. Coarsely chop the cherries, ginger, and pineapple and stir into the mixture. Sift the flour, baking powder, ginger, and cinnamon and stir into the mixture, adding enough of the milk to give a soft dropping consistency. Spoon into the greased mold and cook in a preheated oven at 375°F for 45 minutes to 1 hour. Test by piercing the top of the cake with a cocktail stick: it is cooked when the stick comes out clean. Remove from the oven, let cool for 5 minutes, then turn out onto a wire rack to cool completely. To make the glaze, sift the confectioners sugar into a bowl, then stir in the lemon juice and 1–2 teaspoons boiling water until the mixture is quite runny. Using a teaspoon, drizzle the mixture over the cake. Decorate with crystallized ginger pieces and glacé cherries and serve immediately, or transfer to an airtight container. The cake will keep for up to 1 week, or can be frozen for up to 1 month.

an eas

⅔ cup sweet butter

¾ cup sugar

2 eggs

2 oz. glacé cherries

3 oz. crystallized ginger

3 oz. glacé pineapple

1⅓ cups all-purpose flour

½ teaspoon baking powder

1 teaspoon ground ginger

¼ teaspoon ground cinnamon

½ cup milk

light lemon glaze

1¼ cups confectioners sugar

juice of 1 lemon

to decorate

4 oz. preserved stem ginger, sliced

4 oz. glacé cherries, halved

Makes 1 cake,
9 inch diameter

d-fashioned cake recipe

just like **granny used to make**

Ginger shortbread
with orange and lemon zest

Everyone loves shortbread—made with cornstarch or rice flour to make it especially crisp. You can cook it in a round tart pan, cut it into rounds with a cookie cutter, shape it into a circle with your hands—or use this long slim tart pan so you can cut it crosswise into cookie bars. Ginger has always been a favorite flavoring for this classic, but you could also use all sorts of other flavorings, such as nuts and spices.

2 cups all-purpose flour

⅓ cup cornstarch or rice flour

2 sticks salted butter, softened

½ cup plus 2 tablespoons sugar, plus extra, for dusting

4 oz. crystallized ginger, roughly chopped

grated zest of 1 lemon

grated zest of 1 orange

Makes 16

Grease a jelly roll pan, or a rectangular tart pan, about 14 x 5 x 1-inch.

Sift the two flours together in a bowl, then rub the softened butter into the flour until it resembles fine meal. Stir in the sugar, ginger, orange and lemon zest, then knead until the mixture forms a soft dough. Place the dough in the greased pan and push out to fill the corners. Using a knife, mark the dough crosswise into bars.

Bake in a preheated oven at 350°F for 45 minutes, until pale in color. (It will still be soft to the touch.) Cut the shortbread crosswise into bars while warm, then dust with sugar.

When cool, turn out onto a wire rack and when cold transfer to an airtight container. The shortbread will keep for about 1 week, or freeze for up to 1 month.

Index